HUMAN STAR

HUMAN STAR

SARAH MENEFEE

Sarah Menefee

FACTORY SCHOOL
2005

Human Star by Sarah Menefee
First Edition, Factory School 2005

Heretical Texts: Volume 1, Number 4
Series Editor: Bill Marsh

ISBN 1-60001-043-1

Some of these poems have appeared in: *Split Shift*, *Papertiger*, and *Zenbaby*; and the online magazines *Big Bridge*, *Poetry for a New America* (LRNA website), and *Poets Against War*. 'All Along the Tigris River Bend' was a featured online chapbook on Big Bridge; and 'You Have No Name' was published in chapbook form by Numa Luta Corporal Press.

Cover art: Soheyl Dahi, Untitled, Mixed Media on Paper, 2001
Production Assistants: Octavia Davis, J.R. Osborn

FACTORY SCHOOL
factoryschool.org

Contents

there's nowhere to go

there's nowhere to go:

it's a family you can't leave

gods are built out of the ardor of mystery

tray of loaves on the head of a boy in Baghdad

the man with the missing fingers held up saying

: this is a repetition with a gaping open end

rose

why does it all go rattling off into the night of war and destruction?

nothing but an abandoned and stripped rose left of the bush of them
so full of voices

a sold and resold thornless one

dark age

we are entering a dark age said my son

with this war they begin it

they have been doing it all my life

some of it we remember

an old woman's poor limbs

crippled into a tiger cage

times a million again and again

the night before I woke with a cry

my limbs and the world electrified and hallucinogenic

bodies scattered in the streets

all these years: another autumn

the long nights coming on

disabled veteran & wife

married two years

trying to survive

I see people sleeping in the doorways my lover says

don't they get cold and sick?

they die of it: pneumonia and emphysema

abandonment and despair

a very long torture: pushing and hiding and curled-up exhaustion in the red tents of suffering

the maimed and burned and frozen stretch angelic wings

up toward the pearl of the moon

and the ruby of the rising sun

the bombing begins

terror comes out of the sky

it's an old nightmare my mother had

about bombs falling and a black cloud overhead

when my older sister was in her womb

and my father off to war

it always falls on someone else

and thus is abstracted

here a picture of people running

with cloth-wrapped bundles of brush

to burn it says

what can we know of what lies beneath missiles and carpet bombs

sent in vengeance name?

it falls far away yet it enters the heart like *a burned child*

the black cloud

the fiery brambles of the poor

the running of the legless to no away

staggered for words for the next chapter of horror

and poorer and poorer the enemy

th' already bombed

but there is no already: there is only this child

caught in the rain of fire

came back

came back from that desert war and were in the streets

my friend reads his poem over the phone: of a dog gnawing a burnt corpse

by a bombed-out gas station at the desert's edge

an image from the news I steal from him

holocausted space you want to stick something in

the river

I cling to crow pleasures

walking along

in the streaming dark river

the Milky Way

•

how many years gone by?

who passed the bullhorn to

the street people

who spoke so eloquently

and the wind came

and took them

and they are the blessed

and there's a river

through my solar plexus

that sweeps me away

aorta aeterna of my heart

its signposts are cardboard

held by shivering angels

they say I heart-sign Jesus

help me survive

two young ones sitting there in mid-

stream

and the old one I remember

sitting beside me

who's been out there

for twenty years at least:

brother silence

hunger hunger

thin in all his

parts

•

the crossbar of the tau

is held by the panhandler

with the twisted legs

painfully standing up and

kneeling down

working the middle island

in the intersection

of two wind tunnels

who did this?

we did

look at the they and see

your own brutal

your own greed

•

oh body

I faint at the silk

of your skin

and the taste

of your foreskin

hunger

thy darling

stinky asshole

pleasure lit up

in the mind

•

bringing up the rear the ragged forefront

halt and forgotten

brigade of the legless dancing

let them shout and say what it is

this river of fire

this space

it was going to be enough: this space

of the turning season: enough but for the pretty young mother

with a child and a baby in a stroller begging near Embarcadero Station

•

"I need enough money for a cup of coffee and maybe a little piece of
cake in there"

why did the wild pink break

> why did the wild pink break
>
> oh why did it break?
>
> Issa

Chester my rap musician friend

is saying as we walk up dark Sansome St

after work *I have to remind myself to keep it simple stupid*

in relation to his art: yes I say

it's ok to repeat whatever the heart needs to keep saying

as long as the slaughters keep on

we'll keep this simple too

a brass band marched down Market in all the thousands of protesters
playing *Bella Ciao*

we so don't desire this endless pain inflicted on and on

this sea of blood

we join in saying: not in our name

oh why did the wild pink break?

it is my child the world breaks for profit

one or a stadium or city of them: our families

with their beautiful faces

it's the same heartbreak

all around the world

there is no way to be simple enought but just to cry it out

or put our bodies on the line

and lay our hearts down there:

how do we say it in our American tongue?

not in our name!

flounder

he sits on the stone seat in the river of Market

and looks into the light

the light changes he said and I feel time

he speaks of the slant of the golden light when the season turns

and it seems the night with its mystery is coming

the light is a veil of life

he speaks of the sidewalk wet in the rain

I think of his words when I'm out in the wet

the occult perfume of cement

I wake up in the morning and call for my mother like I never did before what was that you dreamed about time? that word you made?

he is the pearl in my sight

he sits in the light on Market St

we are all looking for the beloved

we are too drunk but we fall down looking

burning for love not knowing how

broke my heart for him to know

the hurt of the little things of the world the innocents

in the world

the earthly paradise

what is the work?

what is the job?

earth sweating earth shaking

you have worked too long on Market St he said

don't I just know it

help me and Petey get through another day

the pitbull Petey with his pink nose

peaceful homeless dogs

down at the side of the human river we weep

we hurry around looking for lunch

there is the flounder on her bed of rice

oh am I its wife?

I put my finger in that honeypot he said and keep tasting its words

I've lost mine: go picking and scavanging for any you drop

through the middle of life: oh am I its wife? so alone?

valentines

a long evening with some late perfume

●

who is the young girl with the black eye?

oh it's me! my feeling of shame

●

dirty girl walking in front of me with your filthy ankles and thin bit
of dress

now I can smell your young stink in my dream: or is it my own?

●

death oh death where is your mother and father?

march

one kneeling one standing all wind long

anything will help: even a smile

the only leg he owns is all fucked up

•

I put my head on his big strong thigh to rest and for love

Violet & April

all my little dramas: the same human one

as time is eaten up: they settle in the gathering flesh

and become as any body is

once upon a time it seemed like a message of pain

sent down from stars impossibly high

the crackings of the impossible self

as the world does crack: as liquid fire cracks it

as emotion is

as the world breaks apart along impossible seams

●

I remember who I was: I was a bully: it wasn't a childish thing

it existed with the world: there were poor girls named Violet and
April to push around

Violet with her homemade dresses the hems turned up raw in front
with big uneven stitches

we forced her to crawl across the bus depot floor

●

the ugly fifties were dying and a new

decade coming with its wars

Violet's dark and handsome daddy drove a cab

standing downtown next to it: couldn't earn enough to feed them all

I would marry him over and over

her mama and all the kids

a baby at her breast

she had no teeth: gumming her stewmeat

spitting the dry lumps out

we sewed and ripped out stitches

frayed and straying edges of all my

images: washing our hair

in the summer rain

in the low-income flat-tops

•

let it go girl you are not a girl you are a length of sky and its screaming lights you were there with your brothers: that long agony and its delights

the frailest human thing:

when everything is gone

the wit of the powerless

our dirty little songs

love for the redhaired boy

youth with pimply faces

pure and troubled lights in their eyes

spoke to me last night

I have loved you forever oh my brothers oh male words

the caves

up to the burnt-out caves of blackened chalk

'Saipan, 1944'
George Herman

over the phone my father reads his poem

about poking thru those ash-lined caves: finding blackened bodies
and bits of bone

his first day there

whose bones we stir I hear

I remember two little sepia snapshots he or somebody took

one of such a burned-out hole: I understood then as a child

that people had been incinerated in there

the other of a family in front of a small hut

the smallest boy with no pants on: his little weenie dangled down

•

if the eye of the soul is a child's eye: oh god

if we saw it so young: what could we do

but go on living in the crystal stream of pity and pain

•

you my friend who were carried out a child of one or two

from a newsreel of falling bombs: screaming

you know saw already totally

and that must be snuffed out

by power

and never will be:

•

the most terrible were the caves he said

all through those islands

entered by the flamethrowers' fire

he said there is no end to what man does to man

man is a wolf to man: Rouault of the hanged man

that haunts the eye of my heart

who wouldn't back way back into oblivion

'as'

what is the marriage we make

in the tenderest lavender of

the twilight's east?

and all that needs to be said

will be or nothing said

but life itself suddenly obvious

holes came holes came   a ripping

what was coming through?

a stillness

not but the light of the existent

name forgotten

story forgotten

it is not madness

you are still able

to do all you need for survival

you don't move and the world isn't moving it is disappearing

and there as ever

we are in the globe of breath

here together

nobody gets to leave another

so full of light

on this day abandoned

you know how unaccountable they are

just by being out there looking up

into their real faces

that they are all about seen and unseen

if you could hear them

and why such few compulsions

as if one word sets the course of life

so the word *whore* becomes the clue for love

in the streets of the world

where everything's sold

an open exchange of fate

around a corner

•

a tearing of

the breath

or would you say *tear*ing

and yet and yet

how do I get up

to the green heart?

•

a porter of ten

running bent with bare feet

under our greedy burdens

lays them down

joins the children in their serious play

as they create the world

a boy with a tray of sausages

in rubbled Baghdad

•

the ruins we create

trying to stop the rose from its blossoming

and the breath and the heavenly rain

•

if I could go below that dreaming place

wanted to divide her ashes and toss them various places

what have we done?

•

that is not to describe the tenderness

of the heart's first love and its boundlessness

and how that was your body

materia mater new and pearly

earth beloved

orgy

yes it was a dream like that one the orgy

naked protesters rolling around in rose petals

don't tell me it was not it went on and on

that those out there set themselves on fire

remembering how the monks did then

still pushes its drunkeness down the Tenderloin

screams from its wounds

you idiot

you idiot you're just as much of an idiot in your dreams as in the day

the whole drama revolving around that

I went howling in pain through the streets

the stage for something that isn't even loneliness

it has become as they say another day

it has its weathers but not much variation

when I came to the sidewalks had the same edgings of pigeonshit

right now stained that pastel green but there's no longer any association

call it forgetfulness though I can still remember

•

when the rains come it's like time is gone

the day liquidly blends into the twilight

and into the night with its voice

I really don't know how to make it into a story

though sometimes a momentarily conscious one begins to emerge

•

the other morning I had a baby the size of my palm crawling around saying
things

and the thing I remember it saying was:

get drunk early and avoid the plague

I asked my friend what kind of bad message that was

and he said not a bad message: just a message

I wish I could remember the last dream somebody told me

now why do I keep leaving out the second m in remember?

maybe it's the forgotten part

•

I heard the words *amor fati* recently and that's what I've been thinking

it's better to be looking at something from a bus when you're thinking

noticing hair everyone moving together

that's something profound and out the windows

•

for a few days it was wonderfully rainy

in a way where the sky is dark and the streets dark and wet

the twisted little arms of the sycamores flailing around

rusty wet leaves plastered against the sidewalk

John tall and gaunt with lovely big eyes huddled against the glass wall
of McDonalds

but what was today? a very quiet a dead Sunday downtown in the
financial district

•

what's a deep and busy dream if you can't remember?

just a feeling that has an edge of satisfaction or comfort the warmth
of sleep

nothing to say till you can walk out into the cold day

with the light coming down from the sky

and maybe some seagulls up there on their strong wings

•

for a couple of years I was waking and saying mama or help me god

that is what has come to me this year that's about to end

•

the taste of the tea is of leaves

steeped like an old puddle you would see in late autumn

and it would feel this way in your mouth

•

I look it in its one eye and breathe its warm perfume

•

I remember the dream where we finally fucked and afterwards

I was in his bathroom sitting on the toilet his semen coming out

like any moment afterwards marvellous that it has happened

•

lots of people are in the streets

a middleaged woman older than her years

with dyed red hair opens the door of the fast food joint for me

going in and coming out

•

it's Monday night no it's Tuesday

the winter solstice is coming up real soon

I recently saw Orion very sharp and bright in the night sky

it felt like getting a look at someone you love and desire

naked that moment you're always waiting for or thinking about

and it's the only moment that exists

that's what you most remember about it

September 13, 2001

I lost my daughter

been said before

one is left in a rubbled place

with a sign: *already done*

on this

very corner

what dusty street in what

poor land?

ask in a rare silence

as my friend does:

what of a burned

child?

what worth

the pearl

of innocence?

what god

of bloody gouts

asks for the burning

of the child?

•

has already

and sleeps on the parched

ground

in a long-blasted place

a boy of eight

dead of pneumonia

naked body lowered

into a hole dug

in the rocky ground

into the poor dry

dying mother

oh mountains!

what poor

place?

•

where is a book

with sayings

such as *in the land*

of the blind?

asked a lovely young

arabic-looking

man

inside whispered:

listen

my younger

sister

went home

in tears

what is the light

what is the light we wake to this October first?

are we awake?

did something change?

the machines are massing in the poorest of places

and terror's the word indeed

get on with your money it says

the blood that feeds it an oily black

don't wash a wound with blood it says

on the side of a bus shelter signed *Rumi*

late at night in the fog

on these dead streets

why so lonely all this life?

doesn't any one but the poorest of poor

appear to you? he asked

of course they do but these

have always been my North Star

an eye above

the lost streets

and deserts of war

and here he comes

the shining of his metal

crutches his pale

face

to him belongs the night

all cold long

cold cold our might

where is the sufic petal and its

black light?

three

in the dead of night

at a quarter till 5 am

an anguished call from a man

I'd been with a couple of times

I just had such a dream of you

it was so kinky I can't tell you about it

can I come over?

oh no I can't *I'm bleeding*

oh god

I fall into troubled sleep:

he is below my window calling

I look out: *there are three of him in a circle*

I wake up in a panic

I'm falling into a featureless place

of my own lovelessness

when you run out

of things and things

to say

somebody else will

or will there be another way?

is it just gathering age

as we say *twilight gathers*

that makes me hesitate?

I stopped and then I went on writing

there is the mystery of the one as three calling up

do they mean *wake up*?

my mind let go and there was a circle

I looked down in wonder

I woke in a panic

who calls?

oh world what is this cell?

does honey drip from its walls?

the mother and father folded their love and anguish in there

day of the dead

over streets where no life stirs

•

back down into our trench of blood

•

two wounded people lie side by side at peace together

•

now they're given back to the mother

•

the terror of all the worlds

•

think of those two hues!

december

if I didn't sit in this cafe with a view of the intersection my writing
might be different

just when I think it might I see him

dark in the dark rain

•

can you tell me how heavy that is?

•

why do I love this desperate wet ass-end of the year?

•

I wanted to buy a light citrine but the rain ran the jewelry-sellers off
the street

•

walking half-dead with shame through this great state of terror

•

a moment of silence for those being crushed and blasted now

•

the year dies tortured burned and cold

•

sparse and shaking stands alone

•

oh dark and purple light!

•

solstice storm comes knocking

what is new and arising

the child: what the human is

in its flame of terror and delight

that the sexual contains

all the little teeth collected in my dream

a pile of bones

a rendering of radiant flesh

oh god oh god

when the world is rubble from horizon

to horizon

the destruction of places people live

the future damned

body holds onto innocence

beyond the mind

•

a hand is held out over my writing journal: in this corner

he wants *a Big Mac fries a cherry pie please in God's name*

reduced to this: and I'm back to my obsession:

a few coins: *give me a dollar for godsake*

the weathered arm a twist of veins: of nature

battered around

of the shame of war and the humiliation of beggary

and my shameful words: *please don't harass me* in

my writing corner

is it a cliche to say

in the midst of plenty?

is it cant?

I can't get onto any other thing

his shame and mine

in the shattered collective

this heartless abundance

invisible strategies of artificial lack

•

there's an organism

a human form: Adam Kadmon

being born: under the spell

of an ogre: disguised

as golem in

its mental hell

•

humiliations: what power can do to flesh

an invisible cloud that swallows

what's innocent:

everything smirched and open

trusting and unashamed

•

a young mother

standing on a bus: her baby on her hip

seeing a smile shine thru

like a spectral sun

kisses its soft cheek over and over

loving as all life does all that is new and tender

and arising

human star

we're all subjected to their *good work*:

the poor tormenting the poor

for power's sake

it's an old familiar scene in domination's

underbelly: *this is what we do*

with all the subjected humiliated

and dead

innocence gagged inside the lyncher's hood

she was lounging against a corpse with long fingers

and a gaping mouth: sadist death

a joke

smoking a cigarette

hoods! torture! how ridiculous! said

sneering Rumsfeld

before we saw

what a brave young soldier

slipped under a door

black executioner's hood pulled over the sweet sun

above the head of sneering Rumsfeld

is the human garbed as a black star

in cloak and hood:

his fine-drawn feet below

a pyramid of bodies

human star tethered there

by electrocution's wires

if you fall through this night

you will bring down

the whole rotten prisonhouse

bury the devourers in the suffering earth

in the holes they explode in her breast

human suffering star!

shame? it's naked brutal power's shame

as though these beautiful cocks and backs could be a shame

to any but the obscene

where the powerless with blood on their tongues

humiliate their own

in master's name

that's how it's always done

and here and there are mothers' sons unlimbed

left poor and legless

to a life of pain: here and there

the poor boys show

their stumps:

the long nightmare

again

box

what you saw locked into that box

the hooded one: that black hood clamped over your own

•

someone's darling on his lap: head thrown back in a swoon of fright

daddy's got a black hood on: incarcerate his little heart

you have no name

hungry to see each other's faces: close your eyes it's a common star

the war inside and out

----

an antiwar sign was out there all the time:

said very hungry please help

those that aren't locked up are out there scattered abruised

----

these incarcerations for which the sun bleeds

here where a paranoid god who lived on birdshit dwelled

has dropped his latest explosion like a turd

---

do we kill there: in sight of such lovely rocks?

---

give me back my own part of the greed

it comes from this desart to far away

---

screams from the human cave

what does it mean to say peace? this palpable light? the emptiness within?

is it a hollowness or a brokeness?

_____

who wanted this? fear did

_____

it's all a pressganging one way or another

every young soldier's an unknown

and hands are washing and washing

do we triumph in the capture of this skeletal naked man?

is that Eden over there into which death is flung?

'even down in the western desert'

I am buying Hafiz a woman said today: I'll take him home for peace

---

an ocean of grief a cosmos of grief

the Red Sea is red and the Persian Gulf

terror: terrified

are you safe in your machine?

––––––––––––––––––––––––––––––––––––

they steal the little one's limbs

––––––––––––––––––––––––––––––––––––

when they attack us I burn I burn

•

I keep stopping and starting again

stepping thru the rents in the world

out there selling roses in the twilight in the cold

---

there's nowhere to go: can you leave behind your wound?

everything's ripped away and confiscated: here at home

---

human being: need help god bless

oh life! you have no name

all along the Tigris River bend

a child draws the Tigris River running red with blood

---

a child mangled and dead: a child crying and burned

bloody little legs dangling down

---

more bombs more bombs all along the Tigris River bend

a mutilation without end

•

the face of imperium: this smallest infinite death

waved a severed hand he found calling Bush Bush

in this holocaust that boils up

clots of plague in the eyes and tar in the mouth

I am twelve years old: armless in my bed

my mother dead my father dead: twenty of my family dead

---

bodies gathered in a blasted land

buried their darlings in the dry ground

shamal: Arabic: sandstorm: pulverized hearts

the merchants of hunger are the merchants of death and destruction

humanitarians: we bring you cholera and diarrhea

---

his wife bombed dead his little wounded girl

there is a weeping that swallows the world

---

shot him in the eye: how does such pain die?

three men crying with bleeding wounds

•

a tank crushes my life: my poetry is broken

---

they break the sweet date palms

kicking to live

a little spark of life in every body

kicking to live struggling to live: unkillable desire

coterminous with the great starry stretch of it

the light of day: that gentle fire